Each poem has Rachel Levitsky's voice in it, but the voice is commanding, demanding you in a sexy, provocative way, urging you to travel with her into a plane that is sonic and wry and physical and unknown. And, you let her. Guide you into language.

—VI KHI NAO

Neighbor is a sweet saga of disconnection. A collectivity of loss. Rachel should be working for the city of New York. 'I've decided to use my obsession/with my neighbor as the context/for a discussion of the State.' That in itself is incredible.

—EILEEN MYLES

Meditating on and inhabiting a wide variety of disciplines and ideas—from architecture to religion, the state to the domicile—Levitsky draws many unexpected connections, sometimes to dizzying effect.

—*PUBLISHERS WEEKLY*

Nearly touching are the ethical realm of our obligation to others and the aesthetic world of our freedom from such obligations. Levitsky's *Neighbor* confronts this imaginary dividing line—in the process, creating a poetry that both provokes community and critiques our social habituations. This is my neighborhood.

—CHARLES BERNSTEIN

In and outside the window of Rachel Levitsky's apartment lie sadness, amusement and conflicted regard for the weirdo constructs of faith and scum politics. Her poet energy is a sweet intellect with lazy compulsive lines dropping onto a free and wishful page, ok with semi-resolve amidst the minor clatter of daily lust.

—THURSTON MOORE

Neighbor
© Rachel Levitsky 2009, 2020

ISBN 978-1-946433-38-1

First Edition, 2009
Second Edition, 2020

Ugly Duckling Presse
The Old American Can Factory
232 Third Street #E-303
Brooklyn, NY 11215
uglyducklingpresse.org

Distributed in the USA by Small Press Distribution / SPD
Distributed in the UK by Inpress Books
Distributed in Canada by Coach House Books via Publishers Group Canada

Typesetting by GoodUtopian
Text set in Bembo, with titles in Avenir and News Gothic
Cover art by Carey Maxon
Cover design and additional typesetting by Paige Parsons
Printed and bound in the USA by McNaughton & Gunn
Covers printed offset at Prestige Printing

The first edition of this book was funded in part by a grant from the
National Endowment for the Arts. UDP is grateful for the continued
support of the New York State Council on the Arts.

RACHEL LEVITSKY

NEIGHBOR

NEIGHBOR

in mind with kari edwards (1954-2006)

CATASTROPHE, UTOPIA

City built in frames framed by these
lines that signal generally good stingy
feeling irony dense and strong as stench
friendly sewage stairway news awaits.

Born can't despite ourselves stay up late
intoxicated but deep reason regret ourselves
days we miss under bleeding sun a shroud.
The princely house faces its other side.

My Neighbor, or Agora

NEIGHBOR

Neighbor is a long page
about the neighbor

why it is called "Confession"
or if it's called "My Neighbor"

or what, if anything, I am.
I have ideas.

At the time I type this
I've been at it for one year

the last six months
completely in my head

where there are many levels.
The problem is whether they

are connected or if
they are levels

at all. "A level" may connote a
piece in a unified structure,

or unity of disconnected parts
firmly housed. By what?

The State or me
or if I am the State.

I am a collection
of desire

precariously
housed.

And so there is Neighbor
and then there is my neighbor.

In the book called *Is My Neighbor*
I am the object

of the relationship I'm in
to which   I have distance.

(between walls and / or levels).
Distance is domain.

I share *it* with the I
of I   that I

am aware of. When I confess
I make this distance.

I nearly wrote detachment
but it is not detachment.

Detachment is the thing
I create when I

am not aware of the I
I am aware of.

Detachment is the thing
I make when I love.

Love is a more complicated thing
when I am speaking of my neighbor

who knows I've rejected him on numerous occasions
to whom I've been lately inexplicably nice.

Love is a complicated thing
when I speak of my neighbor,

crazy, though committed to the logic
of life, currently of being a good mother.

Why do I say then
she is crazy when

crazy is the name used
for those who refuse.

But I love my neighbor
I am sure I

love the closeness / mediated
distance we collaborate / corroborate

I wrote distance not detachment
we never attach / to begin.

Already I am telling you about the neighbor
who today asked   *where was I going?*

Sly look in his eye—
          Which naughtiness are you tonight.

SACRIFICE

It matters this disaster began with an idea.

★

I am thinking about the secular.

★

Yes, I sex my neighbor.

(e.g., curiosity engaged / not
now / slaughtering
each other / not face
to face)

★

When she enters my apartment
she steals from me.

I report her
to the police.

Neither the police nor I care much
to catch

Neither the police nor I
want her

to go
to jail.

*

what we care about
what we don't know

what we don't know
what we build between

*

muscular shoulder / lift in the window / lit / yellow

*

Our hours differ.

*

we want more from each other
we can't stand to not have what the other one has

we can't stand what the other one has
we can't stand the

*

action of light
of waking

★

We are scared   we
could reach   through

shaft, let touch the tips
finger and flank

instead   sacrifice
live things

down   thrown
hard into alley

prayer valley
paper valley.

He could be me so
rapidly I sacrifice

another. They are
small. They

are bugs.

★

It is too easy
to write.

NEIGHBOR

Before I get distracted
(I am easily distracted)

I will try to speak explicitly
on this project, for

at this moment
there is a need

to write directly
into political context.

I am in the United States
which calls itself America.

United Statesians known as
Americans, and Canadians,

Canadians, Mexicans
                    Mexicans.

★

I must write
directly on this page.

I want to say speak
but I am writing

as a United Statesian.

As a writer,
it's more appealing

to treat myself as object
         than subject.
As subject the project

is memoir or
book of reflections.
Either is dull.

I've decided to use my obsession
with my neighbor as the context
for a discussion of the State.

I confess this isn't the only thing I want.

RIGHTS

The poem
is complex and the place made
          in our lives
             for the poem.[1]

Neighbor and I got
bombed / got

oil refinery / four
workers / fallen spears.

No one seems to mind much.
For the sake of empire

cruelty / doesn't require
consideration / imagination

★

He holds forth
I allow him, I look

to him   as the father

return home wander
walls open window my

world   you

Neighbor, rite to this war
these / mean stupid greedy

---

1. anon. — could be me or another, found on a scrap of paper.

outside   low heavy
shady / apocalyptic / kind

We get the oil
                    burn more

I am no lover of
religion.

★

Across the street
food pantry

so important
to imagine

living in the suburbs.
To consider living subjects.

★

Of the difficulty
in the secular

the banal
desire / for a house.

An apartment can only absorb
so much.

★

That church across the street makes me feel safe and keeps the rents low.

Win / Win

Not speaking of religion.

TO LONELY

Bad singing, across the shaft. She hasn't got a pretty voice. He drops off the paper. Sweet so I forgive him, wondering why my box rattles him so.

In the hallway wandering I take him in order to love her. Upstairs in my bare pad we speak … of closet design? The shelving? Bed. No one offers to sit nor drink the water. I regret it, this pathetic muttering over space / division / simultaneity / the possibility I imagine we share by mere misplaced projection here where neither object nor lust arrives along the entering.

FLOOD

My phobia around flag
begins with Neighbor's

collection by which
any flag will be this room-sized

Nazi hung in the basement
conspiracy near

laundry done and
sex illicitily had

not meaning to harm me
nor my fellows so meaning

what. I let him in late one night I mean
to tell (I know this is a confession)

the truth: how many chocolates or
dangerous sexual partners,

the incest, with my neighbor,
the drugs, the high cholesterol,

my embarrassed gender,
that I want this to be a novel.

Everything has to do with the water!
The emphasis on the glass.

BORDERLINE

On the nightly news they interview us about the neighbor.

We say we never expected him. To do a thing like that. He seemed like
a nice guy. He was quiet. Good to his moms. Went to shul on Friday.

He kept to himself but always gave the mendicant a dime.

The mendicant's story is another.
He always knew. There was something off
about that guy.

The guy never "went" crazy,
was the same the whole time.
I knew him.

Which is why
I never called
a second time—

not psychic
but with

good enough
intuition

called his friend
instead

to invite him
over. I'm

not explaining
the voice.

★

She goes onto the TV
with her story:

Being the victim
of a heinous crime—
        (surviving)

circumventing the reason
not to tell.

HOMELAND

There is a public crisis
war on the others
with the planes
from our store.

Maybe the neighbor
cares   but here
is her baby.   She sees only
it. Who has made her.

My miracle, she says,
I sing for him   he
is my   only
song. That's something.

I am the neighbor
who calls to the neighbor: Hey!
My window's broken—
could you lower your voice?

But cannot interrupt
his snoring, for that is
the job of the lover
on his other side.

Can they help it   the people
in that country   we bomb.

Can we help it the people
in this one that bombs.
Someone says general strike
now there is a good idea.

Would the singing mother
join the strike. Are the
bombed babies far away
are they able to help it.

Would she strike her child.
In the night does the cat act
like a dog. I suspect I've
been up for hours.

The bottle collector's
fastidious with black
plastic bags, strewn widely
upon the sidewalk.

The bellowing now stopped.
Has she gone away?
Has he stopped drinking?
Did he get a job?

Is it a boy is it a girl
Is it in the country that bombs
or the one bombed?
Or the other one.

DAWN

I miss my nasty neighbor.

Who talks loudly late into the night on the phone, when he
is not snoring.

But he was quiet, so I slept well after being tired. I mean to
say I didn't do many drugs. Therefore this morning I would
like a glass of wine. But I defer, to the job. I have a job.

This enrages him, the dress, my pretension.
He hears me, considers me the loud one.

As does she, looking behind her to see who hears this story because in
it there is pussy and cock, in the tale about the girl who wears the most
competent cock, though it could be my other conversation.

Equally loud.

[Sidewalk   curb]

Sidewalk curb

    window to window

    face in

    fire escape

War
    difficult in the city
            forgotten quickly

           school library city hall park

       laundromat

       bodega

       station

NEIGHBORS AND DISCONTENT

I am feeling guilty toward him and him and her.
Of course there is more than one neighbor.

They told me they were thinking of me something about
how long I was missing.

Guilty. I wasn't away resisting the war nor making friends
among them. I've done nothing to improve the state
of the State nor instigate any difference to poverty /
violence / skin / wall.

Screaming below. The screaming household is always
below and always. Shrieks of pleasure scare them

when I go there.
I'm concerned

I don't think the kids will remember their day in the country.

DUSK

Today Neighbor has forgotten my name
while we were fucking.

I think we were.
He called me something.

Teacher.
Sweetie. No.... Teacher.

Make up your mind.

And then snored some more.
I couldn't bear it

I cried out the window.... Please!

On the roof, when I am on the roof
he resents me.

Still we introduce. Both smelling
the fumes both
                    a little unnerved.

I wanted to hug him
I mean that I did.

That gives me a funny feeling
still, to this day. From me

he wants only money
a lawsuit

because my fence
fell on his head.

I confess it was together we cried—
some queasy nationality.

Imago

THE STILLS

Images become still, whether or not they were so when I recorded them. Here I am not discussing dream life, which has little to do with the Neighbor (except for when I incorporate sound and waken).

He remains miraculous, lying on my bed in his yellow light. I open the shade a bit.

The movies have done this to me.
The movies are increasingly still.

Stillness doesn't capture what I mean as sameness. The man standing in the empty train depot below the elevated subway. Two man-made cloud trails emerge a V out from the cirrus screened sun.

Thinking perhaps the war has started. In that spot his yellow safety vest and jeans. Medium dark legs (in sooty jeans) an outline an upside down V, across a track or rail. Matching the immanence of the new war. Still. As the train moves away, his shrinkage is a kind of movement. Though as he becomes smaller, he and his position become huge.

To remember a thing
because nothing has moved.

MY MY MY WHAT A MYSTERY NEIGHBOR IS PROBABLY NOT A PSYCHOKILL-
ER ALTHOUGH ONE NEVER KNOWS UNTIL

On the floor on that side is one one never sees,
never hears. I think I know what he looks like.
I suspect I make him better in the head.

It's too little,
his impact on the air.

I suspect he likes alternative rock
works with computers
and is straight

has had a girlfriend only once.
Maybe he has her now.

Thinking of him begs the question: how much one can
shield away from display past the door.

In Truffaut's *Domicile Conjugal* (aka *Bed and Board*)
there is the neighbor who everyone talks about as

the kidnapper.

One day he's seen doing impersonations on TV.
The neighbors rush him, asking, "But *why* didn't you tell us?"

PATRIOTS

My neighbor probably
is not a terrorist

though I fear
for him   unbearable

today   the red and the blue
          balloon   perfection

against   sad   white
          sweep of gray.

babies in fact dying are
dying in dream.   I

burden her with the
project, burden the

project   dates and frames, places for
          insatiable waves

gold pursuit
          white fighting

the gray bank
          of day.

SCREAM UNTIED SOCK IN MOUTH

He and his wife drink and smoke. Their white and fluffy cat runs past the open door onto their porch when he rages. Today there is a sign, the cat gone missing. Spastic big letters of the grief in the new mother.

As in the time of the war the sky is clear but for billows of coal smoke from the chimney across the street.

Still the time of war, the passengers are confused. What should we do with the bag the lady left on the train. Reused plastic bag with gift inside. Lady come get your bag. Too late, she never looked back. A passenger is rapping his lyrics and another seems to be doing the same, but wait, she's muttering, a message, throw it out the train door, throw it out the train door at the next station, don't touch it, throw it out the door, and a little louder finally, so the Samaritan gets a strange discomfort on her permanent smile.

Five in the morning the neighbor screaming again this time something about not caring about the screams heard earlier in the stairwell. (He doesn't give a rat's ass.) I guess he has removed the sock from her mouth.

I have a dream about her. She brings me a product that makes things red. But I'm in the middle of a poo. So it's embarrassing. We are at the city pool. She has one family member after another coming to get her. In this way it is hard to get the red on, hard to get anything done.

I dream about my cat, who is a wild dog.
Whose behavior is unpredictable.

PUPPIES

I'm tired, the neighbors are too quiet.

I'm lucky for the life on the street.

The baby hasn't yet arrived.

Sweat pouring out of him.

Lovemaking is sometimes gross. Sometimes not.

Each day the sky manifests multiplicity.

Therefore so much happens in a day.

Soon I'll walk out the door.

This will take me several hours.

The details are damning.

Was the rug under my feet or ass?

The one in the hall necessarily speckled and tattered at its edges.

Though he is tattered at his edges and has a facial feature pushing

      the boundary of taste, he is irresistible to women.

The other one sweating reminds me of a once popular cartoon.

The baby has now arrived.

THE WINDOW WASHER

He not only makes a good cartoon, he plays a part in the story. Because of the new order, and rules against certain pleasures and extensive systems of reporting, we are now inside our buildings and are socializing, having coffee, smoking pot, giving advice to our neighbors. We know many of us have tried him, the window washer, the service of his love.

The positive consequence of this development (losing the out of doors, the street incident, the unreliability of the corners, of cats and dogs) is learning our window washer is an honorable man. He distributes equitably among men, women, etc. Offers no pretense, satisfies, uses condoms.

It can still go bad.

We can become those who report on our neighbor. Their noise, their fucking noise.

ITS MOVIE VERSION

You can use most of this
though none of it is necessary
(not even the topography).

Debased of language
I enter an era of the banal
(nothing behind the eyes).

The passive conviction
of the everyday pain
in the heart is a pain
in that area of greatest

Sensitivity is most
open for him
beloved stranger
poised at the window

Asking do you want it
there? I am mute
(we are mute)
return to

Gaze toward another
object not
particularly shining an
uncomfortable yellow

Therefore not a turd.

ENVY

A dream performance
artist has the healthier ego

creates a sublime little box
machine that puts out words as

multi-dimensional objects
spare and multi-use.

(Neighbor directing me to
what a weakling I am

a bad bad speller

excessive use of first person
by friction or play.)

I, the dreamer, am
enviously writing

a sentence knowing
its projection, its constraint.

ENVY

Though he's richer and more famous
he would like to have my horse.

His very approach is at same time
expression of desire, assumption of

superiority, hostility.
My shrinking supplication

implying he ought to
get it better.

Funny, how I humor him
call myself the Dwarf

assuming his art
of nothing.

to confess
one needs

a confessor
plus a clear

sense
of shame

we count
on our

goodness don't
want

to
experiment

INSPECTOR

Because he shames me
I cannot hate my neighbor.

When I'm happy
I rub it in his face.

(Do nothing
about madman.)

I live on a street where
people turn (on) each other

into a theory
what does not return.

The police say let him
stay / sleep it off.

The police
who sleep it off / stay.

★

She and I we (love) fuck well
on the stair.

ENVY

I want to take
a package addressed

to Master Neighbor
from Major Neighbor

open it
know

what's inside her
become insider

exceptionally so
nothing of my own.

In the hallway I hear them
discussing, I am thinking

shut up, shut up
shut up. To their voices

which don't sound like water.
Calvino: Ah, but they can't even talk.

Thoreau: disdain at their dumb
stony cover as something

thrown over a shoulder
to recreate the world

or nature, she a solo
writer alchemical

loneliness into glare
disapproval concession

the relatively free
where he and

she both have
little time, just a

little more than the machine
and with their little extra

machine-like, he buys, goes
to church, spends what she

has made him. Family
poorly done, as in Gorky:

Hell. Carrying contradiction
the undoing which insures

doing it again because
of it being good, good

to avoid (their good
his bad, vice versa, and

he was ready to be really bad.)
Back then to the problem

of Good, and Bad. Agamben:
speaking of changing places.

So why shouldn't I take his package (Freud)
But I wrote god and bad (Freud)

Back to problem of god (Freud)
The violence in dead voices.

Therefore not saying a word.
High droning pitch.

I hang back to get behind her
noise, to watch her, from behind.

Better view
quieter.

Perfect California:
A Family Affair

PERFECT CALIFORNIA: A FAMILY AFFAIR

For David Buckel
and with thanks to Vi Khi Nao

CAST *(all characters may be played by any gender)*

Voice: Heavy and luxurious

<u>Elders</u>
Rational Response: At odds with him/herself
Noetic N. Delirium: The inverse of Rational Response

<u>Youngsters</u>
Sunlight-at-dusk: Slippery
Molly: Morose
Luminous Cravings: Exuberant
Finger-in-the-ear: Masturbatory

ACT 1.

Stage: Simple, blue, with some puffy white clouds. White.
There is a scent, of jasmine. It can be
communicated by curvy grey lines ~~~.

Also optional: An elevated highway
of a distance, a small house
atop a hill, up close. A cat
on the couch and/or (why not two? three?)
in the window or
under a bed and
spreading over
a coverlet.

VOICE:

    (Voice introduces characters as they enter. Loud booming Voice.)

Dreams occur! Predicted. Prettiness, perturbation
equidistant cars on raised highway, bay
gleaming in its
10 AM spot. No one argues with...

    (phone rings)

RATIONAL RESPONSE:

    (to Noetic N. Delirium who is on the other end of the phone with a voice that
    is grave, newly awake, not yet taken by the day, barely conversant but betraying
    a sexual urge. Stage lights remain on Rational, for now)

Good morning
Princess.
I wake thinking
of you.

VOICE:

(Voice introduces characters as they enter. Soft demure voice.)

Dreams occur, predicted, yet forgotten
all prettiness, and perturbation
equidistant cars on this tiny raised
highway, bay-oily gleaming way
past 10 a.m. A child whose face
isn't yet very told.

Nobody argues with....

(the phone rings)

RATIONAL RESPONSE:

(to Noetic N. Delirium who is now on the stage end of the phone with a voice that is aggressive, newly awake, not yet taken by the day but taking it, betraying a sexual urge. Stage turns onto Rational)

Good morning
um um um
Princess
I was dreaming, no I was
thinking of...

NOETIC N. DELIRIUM:

(speaking on other side of stage in the dark)

I have $1,200.00 in the bank and my expenses
are about $1,100.00. But then, of course, there
is the loan-to-be-paid-off. I pretend that I can
pay it off at my convenience. In which case I
am flush with $100.00 today—dinner. Oh and
they raised the rent nineteen dollars and
forty-five cents for bringing the
electricity up to code
after the fire in 6J.

(lights go onto Noetic N. Delirium who addresses the audience)

There was screaming and sirens in sleep—
I thought INSURRECTION and SUPPRESSION
and ran to join them but

they were babies
getting burned

The immigrant manchild
individually accounting
cash facts in
class clash.

Never personal,
just that there
are so many (of them)
and the problems.
They don't relent.

RATIONAL RESPONSE:

Noetic N. Delirium, please come close
Be personal data
You are not my
hetenemiga.
Tu eres mi amor a la distancia.

NOETIC N. DELIRIUM:

She didn't mean it,
it was the how of the
where born. My father grew
up, he did, really, poor.
My mother almost died
in a war and has
discovered almonds good
for bliss and heart.
I mean chocolate.
I mean Vicodin.

She is beautiful but has
abandoned remorse.

VOICE:

Remorse requested!

ACT 2.

(a darkening room where all the cast has gathered as Group)

SUNLIGHT–AT–DUSK:

If you peer at a 42 degree angle,
your feeling state may change.
The butterflies have arrived.
Be quiet or the baby.

NOETIC N. DELIRIUM:

I am concerned about the safety of the creatures
in the sea. It has been so long.
What are they saying these days?
Go deeper.
How long.

SUNLIGHT–AT–DUSK:

Examine the streak of gray. Listen, I haven't
really got the time. I am about-to-have-the-baby.

(falls back into Group)

(a crash, a dong, an eery silence)

GROUP:

What happened?

RATIONAL RESPONSE:

Someone died.

GROUP:

A friend?

RATIONAL RESPONSE:

No, a friend of a friend.

GROUP:

Violently? Internally?

RATIONAL RESPONSE:

It is the repetition that ends all others.
There is nothing to say about it.
Yet we speak of it without address
without saying a single thing.
I have something to say about it.

NOETIC N. DELIRIUM:

Is it boring?

GROUP:

Who died?

RATIONAL RESPONSE:

An immigrant.

GROUP:

A member?

NOETIC N. DELIRIUM:

A moment.

GROUP:

What died?

NOETIC N. DELIRIUM:

A cohesion.

RATIONAL RESPONSE:

> The opportunity for insurrection
> is officially temporarily derailed.
> It was an accident.
> But who died?

NOETIC N. DELIRIUM:

> A friend.

VOICE:

> Remorse Requested!

ACT 3.

(around a table)

NOETIC N. DELIRIUM:

(under Rational Response)

I am talking to myself
not saying anything.

This life is make-believe.
This girlie-boy
is on top of me
making sense—
squandering the
position.

I'm tipping.

MOLLY:

Adjustable disdain and reconsideration
I thought you were a friend.

NOETIC N. DELIRIUM:

Yes, I have never wanted to kiss you.
Your body hangs from the air
heart heavy puppet
antipathetic pants sag
from your ambivalent
ass-hips.

(enter from the right Luminous Cravings wearing a purple or red furry cape)

LUMINOUS CRAVINGS:

> I am seeking
> transitional spaces
> a phone booth
> will do.
>
> Do you all want me?
> Incredible, I love you all!
> Ultimate and indefinable
> image I lay out
> bungee cords around your
> gentle lady waists
> trampoline web to break
> your trusting falls.

RATIONAL RESPONSE:

> Another cup of coffee please
> cream and no sugar, not too
> light. Well, light but not too
> much, not too light, I mean
> to say … am I dark?
> I have something to say about it.
>
> *(to audience)*
>
> This isn't about me.
> Pardon me if I go on like this sometimes.
> It's harder in a dialogue,
> everything gets revealed.

MOLLY:

> Who's listening?
> You are the one who comes too late.

SUNLIGHT–AT–DUSK:

>Take cover there's
>too much information
>in a face.

LUMINOUS CRAVINGS:

>Here it is I have written
>my search for you.
>Before I knew you and
>the thing I told you the first
>time we met, that the shore
>will meet the disappearing line
>and be
>the shore.

MOLLY:

>You mean dividing line
>I know what you are
>it says so here
>I am me because you slice me.

NOETIC N. DELIRIUM:

>Motherhood or drug-induced
>euphoria? How do you know so
>much from a room or a brightness filled
>corridor in city once ancient
>burned over, filled in,
>drilled through, rotunded,
>erased, imaged and longed for
>by ghosts trying.

MOLLY:

>Will you repeat
>your mistake. Stop.

Let me. I will repeat your mistake.
Do you know who the father is?
How is it you display yourself
so indulgently. Not for
modesty but because you don't
use it. Please cover
up your part.

(enter buff figure)

FINGER–IN–THE–EAR:

I love you pretty baby.
I'm gonna get you through the night.
Whenever you need me,
I'll be there.
Just call on me.

RATIONAL RESPONSE:

Please explain morality
in home away from home or
levitating trashy mothers.
No, I don't remember the name of the father!
I am trying to recall something else.

NOETIC N. DELIRIUM:

Am I the father?

FINGER–IN–THE–EAR:

You are my sunshine
You are the apple of my eye
That's why I'll always be around you

MOLLY:

>Another lost opportunity.
>You sure it isn't …
>him?

>*(points a finger at Finger)*

NOETIC N. DELIRIUM.:

>Can't be, unless….

LUMINOUS CRAVINGS:

>Artificial Intelligence
>finger babies in your ear.
>You never heard from him and
>you never.

MOLLY:

>Go to hell.

LUMINOUS CRAVINGS:

>Close the door gently.

RATIONAL RESPONSE:

>Ah come on, it is ridiculous
>to go it alone.
>Knot in the stomach no
>fluttering arm.
>So much death.
>Wait, I think I remember!
>Something like is it something like…
>Patriarchy! the death machine.
>Read Aimee Cesaire's
>*Discourse on Colonialism* please.

GROUP:

    Who died?

VOICE:

    A friend.

MOLLY:

    Remorse requested!

ACT VI.

GROUP:

Remorse requested!

NOETIC DELIRIUM:

(to Rational Response)

You thought you could
—point to death
—walk around
the block
—avoid accumulation

RATIONAL RESPONSE:

You feel too much sun no matter
where, how deep, how dark
how covered in cloud.
Yes, predicted by Bioy Casares in
The Invention of Morel
two suns. It feels like
bugs everywhere during
sleep wait I keep referring
you to men. But I mean
Judy Grahn. "A Woman Is
Talking To Death." Ho ho.

LUMINOUS CRAVINGS:

Cloud domain
for the spirit of the not yet here.
Cloudless is for lovers.

MOLLY:

> I think you mean pink, not suns.
> Or if sun, suns, but not sunny.
> Not funny.

RATIONAL RESPONSE:

> I was talking about the
> weather, who can think of anything else.
> Unless you are on that lonely cloud
> of the not yet arrived. I feel for we, watching
> the clock, cooling the inside, heating the outside.
> Molly and Finger endlessly talking about their
> pink overheated bones
> procreating for the sake
> of spirit.

FINGER-IN-THE-EAR:

> Pink's the inside out.
> The hair that won't grow back.
> Air quality is moisture thicket.
> Waterishness everywhere
> we eat and we cathect with plastico-
> chemical-molted iron grime.
> It isn't the fault of spirit.

MOLLY:

> What about sleep. I can't
> defend political
> suicide against love
> safety surviving
> identity stories against
> getting along or cool

sick plastic hospice ex
ink daughter's coral life
refuge escape hunt flood
surviving being born.
Marrying blood to dust,
studying medieval

intersectional
planting plastic carrots,
breathing in waterish
lead remains where a small
dark circle now–time true
finality our burn.

The Desire of the Writer

BREATH

Complaint city, compliant city
horse / car, plane / bomb
sheet rubs ever warm
flowing toward pigeon

Here he is at home
that's how I keep him
where he won't fuck me
I make him coffee

A wage slave with
an annoying neighbor
our "brotherhood of time" is
too groggy to answer his door

They're confused that someone so heavy
is taken like that
taken by the wind
therefore harder to arrest

What does it mean to be hard?
I am not hard
I made the coffee
I aimed to please

But my way is this
way, of grass rather
than path, light-dark
competition for the soft

at slant between
ancient habit to resist
sun's behind, devil's sweat
blue wispy puffy curly

DEFINING

I will like to write an encyclopedia of emotion:
        addiction at all its levels, taxonomy
        of waking states, their mangling
        entaglement on / of
preceding dreams.

I will identify time spans:
        the effect of age on intensity
        if emotion can be identified during orgasm
        or just before and after
        if, like thinking, it is possible to be without.

For this work I will examine:
        postures of confusion,
        betrayal, denial, rage.

When the studies are collected a cross-referencing system will need
to be developed. I will know:
        if lucky is emotion or
        grace, oblivion
        how they differ
        from detachment

Investigate:
        when
        and whether
        Neighbor
        is in fact
        or feeling
        or a substitute.

He no longer watches me.
Have I made myself *le fou*?

AS USUAL

Though poor the architecture was unusual, avant-garde in its time, an experiment, gruesome things grew inside. As usual each appeared to its own sect and as usual there were the wandering few that stumbled in or rolled by on their class trip. I was one of them. I found the contrasts exquisite and would have sacrificed myself unabashedly but for the very shame I felt at not having a good thing to wear.

In fact I was entering into a feeling of absolute chaos, and had to grab the closest thing I could find. I didn't want to be excluded but my choices caused me to limit my involvement. As soon as I arrived at my destination of a lifetime, this discomfort caused me to want to leave, and so question destiny, the very definition of pleasure, success, ambition. No ambiguity escaped me. Overwhelmed, what could I do? I climbed back on the bus! Where they leered as they do, up the silly skirts of us, we without undergarments, without price.

PROJECTION MAP

Because nothing reaches us, we age angrily, our anger grows fungus under our feet. Can we eat the vegetables grown in such circumstance? The wine, the wine.

We rested on the city because that made sense until the housing, limited, smelled of lives we couldn't remember or imagine. We tried to imagine a world where population was a problem for the very first time. Population, either way, was always a problem.

He became a social scientist because the population of his city no longer supported the solution embedded in idea. Suddenly everyone had the language of expertise and furniture to prove it.

He wanted to be both dirty and clean, unexpected and reliable, so as to make a respectable salary, a family wage for the family he didn't pay for. His not paying stood in for a detachment but was removal.

The wage was a problem because of the women. Apparently they could do it all (it all got done!). Then when the testers came they notoriously failed. Perhaps anyone can build a house upon a house.

After that failure it was nearly impossible to find sex. The women discovered public transportation and restaurant restrooms. Desire transposed to public hygiene and stories. What to do with fetish?

★

It's not really a problem to abandon the self.
The replacement, however.

Because we can't decide on a city,
we mention a name.

Imbued with the weight of the future,
an unknown word.

The joke to violence,
the lick of wound.

The relief
in bas relief.

YET NATURE .

The problem with representational art is the audience is often
uninterested in what you represent.

The advantage of Neighbor as the subject of my rendering is
that everyone has it.

Therefore, as a repesentational artist, I am
at an advantage.

The other universal being nature though the only way to go
there is in battle with blind spot. .

I.e., I only speak of birds in terms of pigeons.
We mutually complain.
(We, despite starlings
loving
upon fire escape)

The neighbor isn't very natural
with her child
when she sings to him
he cries.
No Joe, she says, *It's nothing.*

EARTHWORM/GRASS SNAKE

Because I am writing the book about fucking and loving Neighbor I suspect my lover of fucking and loving his neighbor.

Each comes to its own understanding and then fails. I thought a thing about it then simultaneously fell in love with Neighbor and waited for a man. A man did not come, though winter did and our windows closed. I clawed at the shared wall, wailing, waiting, wondering if I were not mistaken when I thought that love was a thing that could make another better.

Coherence and dissipation organized along the choreography of connection between two or three or however many. I told Neighbor it's all about you, meaning as a person you make a gesture that touches a person, and we are two persons touching. In the world where I am at the center I choose panopticon or horizon or close up. In a world where ones (each and every) dissolve, dew settles on any.

ADULTERER NEIGHBOR

As if the world could ever be split in two:
Sadist / Masochist   Homo / Hetero
Boy / Girl   In / Out   Good / Bad

In the middle are the ones who wreak havoc
with their finger / hunger. Having it all.

A convenient threat heats a marriage.
Connection between likes he is
projecting and nervous
inviting me to where she isn't
in her place. Flatters
where I replace her
in "cool" deviance. Deviants
assured of our perfection. Thinking
this will make them kind.

                    ★

If here most souls were not born to be kind.

For example, it's not kind to sell your wife and children, but you
may be forgiven by a father and reincarnated.

What I call kindness may be a Christian vagary of parallel,
multiplied "forgivings" and substitutions with the damned.

He spoke *crazy* in the kitchen. I was almost certain to take him
on as mine.

I fear I am at the point of annihilating the truth.

The too perfect story, lacking dowager, begging another to
change her name.

BLOTTER

The I of I hasn't got a plan.
Like a famous glass wall on a beach in California,
a precarious hold, no longer
on sanity.

Ah, to not last very long.
(He lasts way too long.)

Life should be interesting. Friends should come through.
Friends maintain.
Drugs, alcohol, cigarettes maintain and
threaten.

Gas heat in the house poses several questions.
The good writing (done in the house) is beautiful.
All (this) flesh is judged.

If there is meaning.
If there is offense.
There is television and we
do not always budge.

There is much we think.
We no longer say.
Housed in archives and codes.

There are supplies that run out and places to buy more. There are lines
and plenty of bodies. Abstract love.

There is a limit to presence.
A limit to what is said.
A limit to taking offense.

There is a solitary woman. Many in solitary.
Magic through that door.
There is a tension.

There's rejection
of the tension.
            (Why go for tension?)

There's brother, like neighbor
born to the situation. There is culture and not.
There's a question. Many.

There's Renee (patience and drool), Melissa (patience, Renee),
Rose (impatience, humor).

There's Bill, Bob, Mike, Bob, Tom. Sweat (discharged) and the
organs (discharge).

There are the tall and the robust.
The old who go their way.
There is every detail that someone may know.

We know our details and dream them or
work them for our paycheck.

Eggs, a list of lovers.
The one who cannot love.
The one with money
keeps it to himself.

There is she who thinks of countries. She who enters cultures,
some languages. In the languages there are many languages
and great detail.

She reserves her language, keeps her details.
So there's a town without a map.

Culture its procreating system.
A country that does not

procreate. There's a guy (or two) who may say
"It will not last."

There's a reason for the writing. There's a reason to be loud.
The feeling desired.
The feeling not achieved.

Achievement or guilt.
Wool pulled over eyes.
Almost everyone
realizing they must pull wool over eyes.

There is Rosmarie, Lyn and Leslie. Bob, Tom and Charles.
And Bruce. Screams which are at times not screamed. The
line that keeps us. Or dry. The line forward that fades and
disappears. A plane that doesn't fly. A computer or another
technology that is not so cheap or easy.

There are men and women in conspiracy.
There's fear of death or loss.

Desire for death to avoid loss. Peter, Sue and Tracy.

There is solitary travel and discovery.

There are women.

Babies and sex and rape, for that matter. Travel, unravel.

There is boredom. There is John. Elaine, Juliana, Lisa.

Renewal and the question. Rites or stages without rites.

Pyrotechnic entertainment. A question. A very long poem.

Fragments and chance. Thinking or ideal. Gertrude and papers.
There are Germans.

Alice as executioner. Jen, Jena, Jeni, Erica.

Israel and its Pharaohs. Kahane, Sharon.

Peace. Abstraction. Commerce. Explosives. The young.
Sex. Perverts.

Leaving then coming.

Women. Some carrying babies.
They have limbs. Lips. Some are thin.

Lists. In the head. Shortages of love.

There is Jennifer, Maggie, Rosa, Elizabeth. Judy. Several.

Borrowing countries. There is land and air and water.

There are rites, yearly or once in a while.

Obligation and boredom.
The chosen, the ignored.
The one who needs my money.
Boredom. Happy, high and fat.

Spelling. Marcella.

Heat in the middle of May. Birds and meat.

Artists proliferating. Julian. Money and a crisis meaning cash.

Systems to ignore.

There is high at 8:00. Wandering in the night.

Nervous for the wandering.

FRAMEWORK

The less you (I) leave the house the more autobiographical
the work becomes. I have given you something—was that my
intention? A confession? No sooner made than over: I have
left the house. In fact, I've gone to Florida.

Soft like a clam in the world of *gusanos* and fake tits. Critical,
yet wanting a tan. Watching judgment and nastiness as it swirls
around and spills. I'm sorry, I said, when what I meant was,
keep your stinking body parts in your aura, this side is mine
and you are crossing the so-called borders, not boundaries as
you've just now defined, or may I correct, touted. Americans
know nothing, even you, with your two kinds of people. You
the stinky kind.

Alone on the beach there is the problem of swimming if you
have brought with you your valuables. As nicely as you ask,
Anyone is a problem, and Any Couple suggests the problem,
as you are alone, the problem is you, who swim on the public
beach while underground.

We "as poets" reject cliché so have a hard time saying "let go"
which is for sure, something we could try. As a poet with a
day job, "bowels" and "vowels" is a joke useful for teaching
English to Spanish student workers whose language carries
no distinction between B and V. Because one intends to
express a category of letters, "letting go" is indeed unfortunate
phrasing for a revelation, worse for a revolution, though does
well to connote the normal functioning of a physical need.

I am ahead of myself.

"But I must return to my narrative." Wrest it back to the first
line of this, spew, log, manifesto, confession—definitely not a
poem!

Not leaving the house makes it autobiographical but by then, I've left the house. To a place outside where I am spying on her, through the first floor window. She's on a chair doing something house-wise. Soon she will have a child.[1]

I've written so far mostly of men. Some women: the one with the nice cock, otherwise the women are underground, i.e. mother born of baby born of scream. The women are underground, in flats, flat, flatly.

Or if I am a woman. Well, I am underground.

But I was out of the house.

---

1. It turned out to be difficult for her, or so I suspected when she became publicly and irrationally obsessed with the movements of her neighbors, which could at any moment cause catastrophe. Years later, after the fertility clinic, she'll be the proud mother of twins.

DEFINING

As a United Statesian I do not think that neighbors in other nations treat each other better, or with more care, but I would rather my roommate were from another country.

In this country, it is not the norm to kill neighbors because they have a different religion; group killing may be a form of intimacy we lack.

The poets are not my neighbors and they are not my friends. We agree that our religion, if we have one, is inconsequential to our relationship, and to our poetry, here, in this country. Poets are responding well to the project I have of thee, my neighbor. They wonder if I am speaking of my actual experience and are titillated by the possibility that this fucking I've spoken of, and drugs, are drugs and fucking, not writing.

My neighbor has made a public stand of his sobriety and his fetish: his daughter who he keeps infantile. It is enough to make anyone squirm. Speaking of squirm, tonight I had a plan to do coke, then come home and write about the neighbor.

Is it richer with windows open and summer rage audible. Today the customer at the food pantry across the street excoriates the lousy church that feeds her. The lapsed born-again blames the hypocrisy of her church. I was hoping for a loss of faith in god.

A story is told about a loud and bothersome neighbor, who explained to the complaining neighbor her predicament: "You're my neighbor, you have to help me!" We laugh at this story. We agree that isn't the way we think of things.

Some mornings I wonder if my reluctance to leave the building is enough reason to ask my neighbor for cream or an egg to make the pancakes.

Language would be easier if we could remove the prepositions but then the objects and subjects would be difficult to discern. Like I said, in my career as a writer—I know it suspect for poets to speak of career—I find myself more attractive as an object. If I am the object then who is the subject? Unnecessary.

★

Unnecessary is happy because she is both nothing and everything.

She is as light as air, if air be light. Anyone wants meaning.

Anyone calls meaning Necessary. Unnecessary has intercourse with Anyone.

Unnecessary puts herself into a position where she can't lose.

Loss regretting her lack of an "e", loses Unnecessary.
Loose feels muscular and achy. No, loose is on Quaaludes.

Loose can't explain why Loss gets laid more.
Nor the draw of religion.

The grown ones who never believed in god are assimilated
aliens on the street and trains. Sad ones whose sadness may get read as Intelligence.

Intelligence likes to fuck but gets laid less than Belief.
Never mind the Librarian.

Librarians appreciate quiet refrigerators.
Librarians have fucked both Belief and Intelligence.

Poorly but A Lot.
A Lot gets mistaken for Belief. God-fearing.

Paganism, Atheism and Monotheism.
Masochism. Ism is at war with Unnecessary.

Ism means Motherfucker. Ism is one mean Motherfucker
Everyone wants to fuck, reading her as Meaning.

Meaning delights in Masochism. Ism is a sadist who doesn't
mind lovers calling to her Meaning, while fucking.

Fucking is the sneakiest fuck of all.
Fucking convinces Anyone she's Meaning.

Unnecessary puts up with Fucking because she understands
Fucking to be Without Malice.

Even Cold Hearted loves doing it Without Malice.
Fucking is inclusive, opposite from Ism.

Meanwhile, despite occasional excesses with Fucking,
Downtrodden rages.

Without the rage of Downtrodden, any neighborhood
becomes Suburb.

In Suburb, any human is a living Subject to the Project /
Great Experiment. Catalogued by Librarian into Food /
Medicine / Style.

The project of secular society is no longer an issue because as
United Statesians we don't often kill our neighbors for their
religion.

DISCLOSURE

In our new order
we process artifactual garbage
transparent. Archetype lost.
Slaves to biography.

Cold suck on roof
lacking detachment condom.
This one discarded indicates
the order of events is wrong,

as each new American school kid
learns how the "Indians" lived,
what to do with husbands and wives,
insanity or insistence, cheap lines to

the morning. Morning sleepy
I thought, well-robed. Degradation
not my fault, I slipped out unintended.
I answered the door.

—For you, Inspector Neighbor.

—Who lately nods and eyes suspiciously.

—Or instructs me through the computer.

—Then speaks my name like a text: "As I Live and Breathe."

—As I live and breathe?

—Ass, genitals, naked belly, bearing all … and you said nothing!

—Inspecting.

I went back to sleep discarding
that old torn robe. Confused now
without it and without you here.
I'm not sure how the story goes.

Bad dreams make me
depressive, answering the phone.
It was you, you said nothing
left me no choice but to

return to those degraded, as myself
to their oozing buckets in the attic
crude letters on cardboard—
condemned, my lovers all.

PROXIMITY, INTIMACY, AFFINITY

There are lines we line up along.
We place ourselves more carefully
than you'd think.

The line that is three points
necessarily goes
forward, however

detrimental
to Neighbor who
placed outside

has become
unrecognizable to who
sells then

moves towards
schism
becomes

likely when children
are only cause
for conversation.

★

When one gets the chance to finally speak with the object of
desire, the longing, now it's broken, should be kept out of the
conversation. Obliterated by the contact, a stake into the heart
of your demonic urge.

I for one have forgotten how to speak at all, so no longer
bother to defend my own reputation. As the levels decrease
in my bottles of booze and the discovery of sleep dismissed.

The people live [as] such [in] big beige houses. Their garden is nice. Nice predicted (I have that song) is not predicated. It is lasting.

Proximity is a curved line that moves to affinity, but affinity isn't intimacy, and intimacy evades in the utmost proximity. So when you say, "we go to church for intimate space," I will say that is because of affinity (the belief in god). For this you need to believe in god, and so we ask, why or why not believe in god. Therefore we make no sense with each other, though tonight we would really like to.

On the other hand, when you believe in god, none of you make sense. You make sense of each other.

★

I for one cannot stop
drinking coffee and

try as I might
to envision

the square upon which
the corners are not churches

I have failed
to replace them.

Notes

At the DC reading Tina Darragh, who shows up now in all my books, talked about Heather's animal log, and I said, "Oh, NEIGHBOR is a log," and she said, "Yes, it is."

Right then in the bar, some others were talking about *Manifesto* and I said, "Oh, NEIGHBOR is a manifesto," and they said, "Yes, it is."

Later talking with G in the car on the highway, said, "I think I will resolve the problem of the poetry by breaking it into lines," and G said, "Yes, break into lines."

Listing the reading: Transcendentalists, René Girard, Jane Jacobs—to which Renee said, "What about *The Making of Americans?*" And I said "Yes, *The Making of Americans.*"

Remaining the issue of time and timing, which is when do I respond to my neighbor as he is acting, or as I am thinking, or later when I have finally found the time to write. For example, I was on the phone with D when I heard the neighbor scream:

Would You Please Turn Down Your Radio

And I thought it was the neighbor with whom I'd linked fingers in the bar, but it was the other neighbor the one who is supposed to have left the gagged neighbor and her child. Or did she throw him out. This issue of who leaves who being the one that is currently / kicking my ass / since I am the one / who is both fleeing and waiting, always fleeing and waiting. Of course he is the loud one / though it's hard to absorb. Remember, he is the one who worries about how his father / would have done it. He was yelling and he yelled again:

Would You Please Turn Down Your God-Damned Radio!

so that D heard and liked the irony.

Then the issue of sentimentality, if you think of this as a log. Or poetry, if you think of it as manifesto. Then the problem of me talking to you in this way.

I was surprised by the way my neighbor talked to me, which was in fact sentimental and lacked irony and defeated much of what I've written about him so far.

He told me he was nervous about coming home with the new baby and wanted to tell me, his neighbor, about it, in the hopes of soliciting my love and support.

Sincere neighbor.

As for the reading, it goes poorly. I discover everyone acts as a discoverer. Like an explorer the discoverer is not so much of a settler though they settle down and by doing so change the neighbor.

NOTES

PLACE HEADINGS (i.e., *bed/studio* et al.)
I took inspiration from Gaston Bachelard's concept of "topoanalysis" in his book *The Poetics of Space* which is popular with poets. I thank Anselm Hollo for first suggesting this book to me in 1996.

P.41 PATRIOTS—At least half the words reordered from Emily Dickinson's poem "A Slash of Blue."

P.56 SECTION III, "PERFECT CALIFORNIA: A FAMILY AFFAIR"—This dedication seeks to extend the life work and political death of David Buckel, who, as a lawyer, fought and won several cases that paved the way for LGBTQAI+ anti-discrimination laws and policies (he was the lead lawyer in a landmark case that recovered damages against neglectful police for the family of Brandon Teena, a trans man that was brutally raped and later murdered in Nebraska on New Year's Eve, 1993), who as a founding laborer at Red Hook Farms' composting program in Brooklyn, mentored future master composters, and finally, who staged a protest suicide at 6 a.m. on April 14, 2018 at the age of 60, two weeks after the Trump regime announced major E.P.A. auto emission rule rollbacks.

The act was framed by him, in a letter he emailed to the media, as a screed against the ongoing use of fossil fuel on a planet becoming inhospitable for human (and many other forms of) life, and as "a hope that giving a life might bring some attention to the need for expanded action."

Despite his methodical procedure and clear statements, some people interpret David Buckel's dire act as solely personal and question its political efficaciousness, both because of the speed with which it passed through the news cycle and because it wasn't enough seen, responded to immediately, as for example, was the self-immolation of Tarek el-Tayeb Mohamed Bouazizi in Tunisia on December 17, 2010, a suicide that visibly catalyzed Tunisia's Jasmine Revolution. But Bouazizi's act occurred in proximity to many political suicides of the Arab Spring that were less noted but which came out of similar exasperations with governmental disregard for human life. Buckel set up his act in the wee hours of the morning, to be unseen, unphotographed.

I was encouraged to learn that Joel Sternfeld, a notable NYC photographer that was in Prospect Park with his child on April 14, 2018, has published a book of photographs he took of the site of David Buckel's death, called *Our Loss* (Steidl, 2019). This note that I'm adding to the second edition of *Neighbor* goes to press on the eve of a major national walk out to save the planet on September 20, 2019...hopefully to be continued.

"PERFECT CALIFORNIA: A FAMILY AFFAIR," was performed by Feed the Herd Theater Company during "Plays on Words: A Poets and Theater Festival," curated by Tony Torn, Lee Ann Brown and Corina Copp at The Ontological-Hysteric Incubator and The Poetry Project, St. Mark's Church, New York, NY, May 11-15, 2006.

Director: Brian Snapp
Assistant Director: Jesse Ann Pirraglia
Cast (in order of speaking):
    Voice: Scott Duprey
    Rational Response: Alexandre Correia, Jr.
    Noetic N. Delirium: Metha Brown
    Sunlight-at-dusk: Katherine Serpa
    Molly: Alexandra Gizela
    Luminous Cravings: David John Peter Smith III
    Finger-in-the-ear: Jermaine Chambers

P.76 YET NATURE—The work of Marcella Durand, Juliana Spahr, Jonathan Skinner, Jane Sprague and many other contemporary proponents of eco-poetics inspired me to finally look up the ever pervasive (outside my window) starling, online where it's easy enough. And so I found out that 99 European Starlings were released in 1890 in Central Park and 15 survived to spawn millions in the years to come. Our starlings push out other birds from their nests, especially bluebirds, spread some disease, eat insects and are hearty urban dwellers. They are known for causing disease to farm animals and causing aviation disasters.

P. 84 FRAMEWORK—The quote is from Proust.

MY GRATITUDE

I had a very difficult time "letting go" of this work and would not have if it weren't for those of you who encouraged me to do so. Thank you. The editors at Ugly Duckling Presse have been confident and enthusiastic about this work since/despite its chaotic beginnings. Their long patience and publishing of this book is testimony to both the political necessity and critical value of community and context in writing, performing and making books. I especially thank Matvei Yankelevich and Paige Parsons, who've worked tenderly with me on this reprint, and Anna Moschovakis, the editor of the first edition. UDP is long heroic in numerous some *unseen* ways. It continues to need our ongoing material support.

Nicolas Veroli, Renee Gladman, Laura Elrick, Leslie Scalapino, Rick Karr, and Gail Scott read drafts. Their responses encouraged me towards clarity and away from indulgence. For Time and Money, I am grateful to the MacDowell Colony, and a Mellon Grant from Pratt Institute. And to Erica Kaufman, Charles Bernstein, Marcella Durand, Akilah Oliver and Stacy Szymaszek for unflinching, meaningful support. This work was mainly written in the middle of the night throughout 2002/2003 (insomniac, trying to quit smoking) and it was messy. I created a complicated architecture for it during the artist's residency at MacDowell in 2004; ironically that architecture prevented me from reentering the work to improve it for several years. On a long train trip to Montreal on my way back from visiting Gail Scott in November 2007 I was able to go in and excise many of the overbearing features of my so-called architecture, and level the text. I don't know if this says something about architecture or not. Rachel Zolf offered me her incredible vision toward editing, and many concrete suggestions which enabled me to work this final rendering.

The following editors and publications published segments of the book that were extensive enough to have context to the larger project, and were patient and artful in their editing: Mónica de la Torre (The Brooklyn Rail), kari edwards and Stacy Szymaszek (Eoagh), Stacy Szymaszek and Corrine Fitzpatrick (The Recluse), Chris Martin (Puppy Flowers), Brian Clements (Sentence), Tom Orange (DC Poetry Anthology), Richard Owens (Damn the Caesars), Marcella Durand (Center for Book Arts Broadside, with letterpress design by Shanna Yarbrough), Virginie Poitrasson (Action Poétique, translation by Stéphane Bouquet), and Eiríkur Örn Norddahl (slög med bilum, translation by the author).